happily ever after

# YOU-NICORN
## Journal

HAPPILY EVER AFTER PRESS

You-Nicorn Journal

Published by HEA Press

# INTRODUCTION TO THE
# *YOU-NICORN JOURNAL*

*This is an excerpt from* YOU-NICORN: A 30-day book to find your inner unicorn and start living the life you love, *by Danielle Vincent, which is available at you-nicorn.com. The* YOU-NICORN Journal *can be used independently, or in concert with the* YOU-NICORN book.

There are no rules about how to use a journal, just as long as you use it with enough regularity that you don't feel burdened by "starting up again." For me, daily is that cadence. If I miss a day, it's not such a big deal. But if I miss two days, I start feeling behind, and like I need to "catch up." Too much happens, I have too many thoughts, and it gets harder and harder to open the journal and just dash off a quick entry. There are several ways of keeping a journal, so if you've tried to journal in the past and haven't found it useful, read on.

## THE MORNING PAGES
Popularized in *The Artist's Way* (a great book, by the way), the Morning Pages is an exercise where you write three pages of *whatever* every morning. It's basically a brain dump of all the unprocessed noise rumbling around in your brain like gravel in your mouth. It's really basic and straightforward: three pages, content is irrelevant, unfailingly every morning.

## WHAT WORKED, WHAT DIDN'T
This one is from my friend Beth. She keeps a daily journal of the things that worked and the things that didn't work. Yep, that simple. I'm sure you can see how this would also be tremendously helpful.

## FREEFORM JOURNALING

This is my method. I carry my journal with me *everywhere* and I work out darn near *everything* in the journal. As soon as this chapter's over, I'm probably going to write about how I'm writing this book, and that it's really hard, and then I'll brainstorm ways to break down the task into smaller tasks (yes, smaller than 30 days), and then hopefully I'll come up with some good solutions.

I write about events that happened, and hopes I have for the future. I write about goals that I have, and I even work out budgets if I need some private scribble-space.

I keep all my journals, because I find it helpful to go back and read past journals.

## FOR FINDING YOUR DIRECTION

My friend Janet and I were talking about the importance of journaling the other day. She is a coach and friend to many people at many points in their lives, and recommends they start journaling as the first course of action when people come to her for direction.

She has a three-question guided journaling practice, which should take exactly a half hour every morning. Each question should take 10 minutes (just set a timer), no more, no less. Even if you have nothing to say, just ramble with whatever comes into your head. That's the nature of journaling sometimes: you just keep rambling, and eventually some order comes around. Or no order comes around, and order comes around some other day. It's all fine.

Her three questions are:
1. What do I love doing?
2. What gives me energy?
3. What unique skills, experiences, and perspectives do I have that nobody else has?

For each of these questions, just answer them every day, the same questions, for 10 minutes each. Over time, you will gain clarity about your interests and direction!

*We hope you enjoy your journal. Please keep in touch at you-nicorn.com and let us know how you like it!*

If you could achieve one thing in the next 3 months, what would it be?

Why is this important to you?

_____

_____

_____

_____

_____

_____

Notes / Doodles / Freeform Thoughts...

TODAY I FEEL:

:D  :)  :|  :(  >:(  ( )

(Fill in)

_____
_____
_____
_____
_____
_____
_____
_____
_____
_____
_____
_____
_____
_____
_____
_____
_____

DATE: _____

GOAL I'M WORKING ON:

DAYS WORKING TOWARD GOAL: ( )

WHY I'M DOING IT:

Notes / Doodles / Freeform Thoughts...

DATE: _____

Notes / Doodles / Freeform Thoughts...

LET'S GO!

Notes / Doodles / Freeform Thoughts...

# PONDER THIS...

Write about a time in your life when things that seemed to be going wrong actually turned out for the best.

_____

_____

_____

_____

_____

_____

_____

_____

_____

_____

_____

_____

_____

_____

_____

_____

_____

Notes / Doodles / Freeform Thoughts...

TODAY I AM GRATEFUL FOR:

① _____

_____

_____

② _____

_____

③ _____

_____

_____

DATE: _____

Notes / Doodles / Freeform Thoughts...

Notes / Doodles / Freeform Thoughts...

DATE: _____

"The best time to plant a tree was 20 years ago. The second best time is today."

- CHINESE PROVERB

Notes / Doodles / Freeform Thoughts...

_____
_____
_____
_____
_____
_____
_____
_____
_____
_____
_____
_____
_____
_____
_____

TODAY I'M PROUD OF MYSELF FOR: _____
_____
_____
_____
_____
_____
_____
_____

Notes / Doodles / Freeform Thoughts...

TODAY I FEEL:

:) :) :| :( :( ( )

(Fill in)

DATE: _____

GOAL I'M WORKING ON:

DAYS WORKING TOWARD GOAL: ( )

WHY I'M DOING IT:

24

Notes / Doodles / Freeform Thoughts...

Notes / Doodles / Freeform Thoughts...

_____

_____

_____

_____

_____

_____

_____

_____

_____

_____

_____

_____

_____

_____

_____

_____

_____

_____

_____

_____

_____

I BELIEVE IN YOU!

Notes / Doodles / Freeform Thoughts...

PONDER THIS...

Write about something you're particularly good at.

_____

_____

_____

_____

_____

_____

_____

_____

_____

_____

_____

_____

_____

_____

_____

Notes / Doodles / Freeform Thoughts...

TODAY I AM GRATEFUL FOR:

1 _____
_____
_____

2 _____
_____
_____

3 _____
_____
_____

DATE: _____

Notes / Doodles / Freeform Thoughts...

DATE: _____

Notes / Doodles / Freeform Thoughts...

DATE: _____

"Begin doing what
you want to do now.
We are not living in
eternity. We have only
this moment, sparkling
like a star in our
hand—and melting
like a snowflake."

- SIR FRANCIS BACON

Notes / Doodles / Freeform Thoughts...

_____
_____
_____
_____
_____
_____
_____
_____
_____
_____
_____
_____
_____
_____

TODAY I'M PROUD OF MYSELF FOR: _____
_____
_____
_____
_____
_____
_____
_____

Notes / Doodles / Freeform Thoughts...

TODAY I FEEL:

😃 🙂 😐 🙁 😣 ◯

(Fill in)

DATE: _____

GOAL I'M WORKING ON:

DAYS WORKING TOWARD GOAL: ◯

WHY I'M DOING IT:

Notes / Doodles / Freeform Thoughts...

Notes / Doodles / Freeform Thoughts...

DATE: _____

Notes / Doodles / Freeform Thoughts...

PONDER THIS...

It's five years in the future and you wake up starting
your perfect day. What does that day look like to you?

_____
_____
_____
_____
_____
_____
_____
_____
_____
_____
_____
_____
_____
_____
_____
_____
_____

Notes / Doodles / Freeform Thoughts...

TODAY I AM GRATEFUL FOR:

DATE: _____

1 _____
_____
_____

2 _____
_____
_____

3 _____
_____
_____

Notes / Doodles / Freeform Thoughts...

Notes / Doodles / Freeform Thoughts...

_____

> "You aren't a bad person. You are a person who has done bad things. But you're not a bad person."
>
> **- RANDI HOKETT, ARTIST, FRIEND, AND ACCIDENTAL SPIRITUAL ADVISOR**

Notes / Doodles / Freeform Thoughts...

DATE: _____

_____
_____
_____
_____
_____
_____
_____
_____
_____
_____
_____
_____
_____
_____

TODAY I'M PROUD OF MYSELF FOR: _____
_____
_____
_____
_____
_____
_____

Notes / Doodles / Freeform Thoughts...

TODAY I FEEL:

😀 🙂 😐 😕 😣 ⬤

(Fill in)

DATE: _____

GOAL I'M WORKING ON:

DAYS WORKING TOWARD GOAL: ⬤

WHY I'M DOING IT:

56

Notes / Doodles / Freeform Thoughts...

DATE: _____

58

Notes / Doodles / Freeform Thoughts...

HIC

Notes / Doodles / Freeform Thoughts...

# PONDER THIS...

Write about a time you felt especially powerful and capable. What were you doing? How did it feel?

_____

_____

_____

_____

_____

_____

_____

_____

_____

_____

_____

_____

_____

_____

Notes / Doodles / Freeform Thoughts...

TODAY I AM GRATEFUL FOR:

1 _____

_____

_____

2 _____

_____

_____

3 _____

_____

_____

DATE: _____

Notes / Doodles / Freeform Thoughts...

Notes / Doodles / Freeform Thoughts...

_____

"*We are what we repeatedly do.*"

**- ARISTOTLE**

Notes / Doodles / Freeform Thoughts...

_____
_____
_____
_____
_____
_____
_____
_____
_____
_____
_____
_____
_____
_____
_____

TODAY I'M PROUD OF MYSELF FOR: _____
_____
_____
_____
_____
_____
_____

Notes / Doodles / Freeform Thoughts...

TODAY I FEEL:

😃 🙂 😐 😕 😣 ◯

(Fill in)

_____
_____
_____
_____
_____
_____
_____
_____
_____
_____

DATE: _____

GOAL I'M WORKING ON:

DAYS WORKING TOWARD GOAL: ◯

WHY I'M DOING IT:

_____
_____
_____
_____
_____
_____

Notes / Doodles / Freeform Thoughts...

Notes / Doodles / Freeform Thoughts...

fig. 1:
turd
sandwich

Notes / Doodles / Freeform Thoughts...

PONDER THIS · · ·

Who believes or believed in you? What was one thing they
saw in you that made them especially appreciate you?

_____

_____

_____

_____

_____

_____

_____

_____

_____

_____

_____

_____

_____

_____

_____

Notes / Doodles / Freeform Thoughts...

TODAY I AM GRATEFUL FOR:

① _____

_____

_____

② _____

_____

_____

③ _____

_____

_____

DATE: _____

Notes / Doodles / Freeform Thoughts...

Notes / Doodles / Freeform Thoughts...

_____
_____
_____
_____
_____
_____
_____
_____
_____
_____
_____
_____
_____
_____

> "Every now and then [I expected someone would be] suggesting to me that such extreme nicety as I exacted of myself be a kind of foppery in morals, which, if it were known, would make me ridiculous; that a perfect character might be attended with the inconvenience of being envied and hated; and that a benevolent man should allow a few faults in himself, to keep his friends in countenance."
>
> - BENJAMIN FRANKLIN

Notes / Doodles / Freeform Thoughts...

_____
_____
_____
_____
_____
_____
_____
_____
_____
_____
_____
_____
_____
_____

TODAY I'M PROUD OF MYSELF FOR: _____
_____
_____
_____
_____
_____
_____

Notes / Doodles / Freeform Thoughts...

TODAY I FEEL:

☺ ☺ 😐 🙁 😠 ◯

(Fill in)

_____

_____

_____

_____

_____

_____

_____

_____

_____

DATE: _____

GOAL I'M WORKING ON:

DAYS WORKING TOWARD GOAL: ◯

WHY I'M DOING IT:

_____

_____

_____

_____

_____

_____

_____

Notes / Doodles / Freeform Thoughts...

Notes / Doodles / Freeform Thoughts...

Notes / Doodles / Freeform Thoughts...

PONDER THIS...

What's your favorite song? Why? How does it make you feel?

Notes / Doodles / Freeform Thoughts...

TODAY I AM GRATEFUL FOR:

DATE: _____

① _____

_____

② _____

_____

③ _____

_____

Notes / Doodles / Freeform Thoughts...

Notes / Doodles / Freeform Thoughts...

_____
_____
_____
_____
_____
_____
_____
_____
_____
_____
_____
_____
_____
_____
_____
_____
_____
_____
_____
_____
_____
_____

> "If you're going
> through Hell,
> keep going."
>
> - WINSTON CHURCHILL

Notes / Doodles / Freeform Thoughts...

DATE: _____

_____
_____
_____
_____
_____
_____
_____
_____
_____
_____
_____
_____
_____

TODAY I'M PROUD OF MYSELF FOR: _____
_____
_____
_____
_____
_____
_____

Notes / Doodles / Freeform Thoughts...

TODAY I FEEL:

😀 🙂 😐 😕 😠 ◯

(Fill in)

DATE: _____

GOAL I'M WORKING ON:

DAYS WORKING TOWARD GOAL: ◯

WHY I'M DOING IT:

Notes / Doodles / Freeform Thoughts...

Notes / Doodles / Freeform Thoughts...

Notes / Doodles / Freeform Thoughts...

PONDER THIS...

What's one adventure you'd like to go on? What excites you about it? Who would come with you?

_____

_____

_____

_____

_____

_____

_____

_____

_____

_____

_____

_____

_____

_____

_____

_____

Notes / Doodles / Freeform Thoughts...

TODAY I AM GRATEFUL FOR:

DATE: _____

1 _____

2 _____

3 _____

Notes / Doodles / Freeform Thoughts...

Notes / Doodles / Freeform Thoughts...

"No battle plan survives
contact with enemy."

- HELMUTH VON MOLTKE

Notes / Doodles / Freeform Thoughts...

_____
_____
_____
_____
_____
_____
_____
_____
_____
_____
_____
_____
_____
_____
_____

TODAY I'M PROUD OF MYSELF FOR: _____
_____
_____
_____
_____
_____
_____

Notes / Doodles / Freeform Thoughts...

TODAY I FEEL:

😄 🙂 😐 😖 ☹️ ◯

(Fill in)

_____
_____
_____
_____
_____
_____
_____
_____
_____
_____

DATE: _____

GOAL I'M WORKING ON:

DAYS WORKING TOWARD GOAL: ◯

WHY I'M DOING IT:

_____
_____
_____
_____
_____
_____

Notes / Doodles / Freeform Thoughts...

Notes / Doodles / Freeform Thoughts...

_____

Notes / Doodles / Freeform Thoughts...

PONDER THIS...

If you could change anything, what would you improve in your life? Your country? Our planet? What's one habit you could put into action every day to make that more of a reality?

Notes / Doodles / Freeform Thoughts...

TODAY I AM GRATEFUL FOR:

1 _____
_____
_____

2 _____
_____
_____

3 _____
_____
_____

DATE: _____

Notes / Doodles / Freeform Thoughts...

Notes / Doodles / Freeform Thoughts...

_____

_____

_____

_____

_____

_____

_____

_____

_____

_____

_____

_____

_____

_____

_____

_____

_____

_____

_____

_____

_____

*"Holding onto anger is like drinking poison and expecting the other person to die."*

**- ANONYMOUS**

Notes / Doodles / Freeform Thoughts...

_____
_____
_____
_____
_____
_____
_____
_____
_____
_____
_____
_____
_____
_____
_____

TODAY I'M PROUD OF MYSELF FOR: _____
_____
_____
_____
_____
_____
_____
_____

134

Notes / Doodles / Freeform Thoughts...

TODAY I FEEL:

😃 🙂 😐 😕 🙁 ◯

(Fill in)

DATE: _____

GOAL I'M WORKING ON:

DAYS WORKING TOWARD GOAL: ◯

WHY I'M DOING IT:

Notes / Doodles / Freeform Thoughts...

Notes / Doodles / Freeform Thoughts...

FABULOUS EXHIBITA:
YOU!

Notes / Doodles / Freeform Thoughts...

PONDER THIS...

write about a time when a stranger was
particularly kind to you.

Notes / Doodles / Freeform Thoughts...

TODAY I AM GRATEFUL FOR:

1 _____
_____

2 _____
_____

3 _____
_____
_____

DATE: _____

Notes / Doodles / Freeform Thoughts...

Notes / Doodles / Freeform Thoughts...

_____
_____
_____
_____
_____
_____
_____
_____
_____
_____
_____
_____
_____
_____
_____
_____
_____
_____
_____
_____
_____
_____

> *"Few people know so clearly what they want. Most people can't even think what to hope for when they throw a penny in a fountain."*
>
> **- BARBARA KINGSOLVER**

Notes / Doodles / Freeform Thoughts...

DATE: _____

_____

_____

_____

_____

_____

_____

_____

_____

_____

_____

_____

_____

_____

TODAY I'M PROUD OF MYSELF FOR: _____

_____

_____

_____

_____

_____

_____

Notes / Doodles / Freeform Thoughts...

TODAY I FEEL:

😀 🙂 😐 😟 ☹️ ◯

(Fill in)

DATE: _____

GOAL I'M WORKING ON:

DAYS WORKING TOWARD GOAL: ◯

WHY I'M DOING IT:

Notes / Doodles / Freeform Thoughts...

Notes / Doodles / Freeform Thoughts...

Notes / Doodles / Freeform Thoughts...

PONDER THIS...

What brings you a sense of stillness? Write about a place
or a time when you felt your spirit was at peace.

_____

_____

_____

_____

_____

_____

_____

_____

_____

_____

_____

_____

_____

_____

_____

_____

_____

_____

Notes / Doodles / Freeform Thoughts...

TODAY I AM GRATEFUL FOR:

1 _____

_____

2 _____

_____

3 _____

_____

DATE: _____

Notes / Doodles / Freeform Thoughts...

Notes / Doodles / Freeform Thoughts...

"*Don't try to understand! It's enough if you do not misunderstand.*"

- NISARADATTA MAHARAJ

Notes / Doodles / Freeform Thoughts...

_____

_____

_____

_____

_____

_____

_____

_____

_____

_____

_____

_____

_____

TODAY I'M PROUD OF MYSELF FOR: _____

_____

_____

_____

_____

_____

_____

Notes / Doodles / Freeform Thoughts...

TODAY I FEEL:

☺ ☺ 😐 😕 😠 ○

(fill in)

DATE: _____

GOAL I'M WORKING ON:

DAYS WORKING TOWARD GOAL: ○

WHY I'M DOING IT:

Notes / Doodles / Freeform Thoughts...

Notes / Doodles / Freeform Thoughts...

Notes / Doodles / Freeform Thoughts...

PONDER THIS...

What does love mean to you and how do you show it to other people? (Not just romantic love, but all types of love.)

_____

_____

_____

_____

_____

_____

_____

_____

_____

_____

_____

_____

_____

_____

_____

_____

_____

_____

Notes / Doodles / Freeform Thoughts...

TODAY I AM GRATEFUL FOR:

1) _____

_____

2) _____

_____

3) _____

_____

DATE: _____

Notes / Doodles / Freeform Thoughts...

Notes / Doodles / Freeform Thoughts...

"The only way to have
a friend is to be one."

- UNKNOWN

Notes / Doodles / Freeform Thoughts...

DATE: _____

_____
_____
_____
_____
_____
_____
_____
_____
_____
_____
_____
_____
_____
_____
_____

TODAY I'M PROUD OF MYSELF FOR: _____
_____
_____
_____
_____
_____
_____

Review your journal and reflect on what happened since you started...

_____

_____

_____

_____

_____

_____

_____

_____

_____

_____

_____

_____

_____

_____

_____

_____

_____

_____

_____

# Did you make progress on your goal?

( YES! ) ( STILL WORKING ) ( NO. )

76291745R00106

Made in the USA
Middletown, DE
11 June 2018